The Reason Why I Sing
2nd Edition

A Book of Lyrical Songs

By
Elisheva Yaakova

FM Publishing Company
Casa Grande, Arizona 85130

The Reason Why I Sing, 2nd Edition
A Book of Lyrical Songs

Published by:

FM Publishing Company
P.O. Box 10744
Casa Grande, AZ 85130-0108
United States of America
www.fmpublishingcompany.com

Unless otherwise indicated, all Scripture quotations are taken from The New King James Version. Copyright ©1982, Thomas Nelson, Inc. Publishers. Used by permission.

Printed in the United States of America

ISBN 9781931671309

Library of Congress Control Number 2011924076

Make a joyful noise unto YAHWEH, all ye lands. Serve YAHWEH with gladness: come before his presence with singing. Know ye that YAHWEH he is Yahweh: it is he that hath made us, and not we ourselves; we are his people, and the sheep of his pasture. Enter into his gates with thanksgiving, into his courts with praise: be thankful unto him, and bless his name. For YAHWEH is good; his mercy is everlasting; and his truth endureth to all generations.

Psalm 100

Introduction

Through our powerful prayers we are able to commune with the Most Holy One of Hosts (Yahweh) and with His heavenly angels. It delights the soul, renews the spirit, and enlightens the mind. This collection of songs was borne out of those prayers and heartfelt communion with His Majesty.

These songs span a period of 33 years from 1987 to 2010. They represent my spiritual search, spiritual conversion, and experiences with various churches, pastors, and believers. They are a collection of my praise and worship from the still quiet whispers with tears and thanksgiving – to the loud, tongue-speaking, hand-clapping and feet-stomping *shabach* times with Yahoshua.

Although I can always hear the music in my head, unlike Mozart, I am not adept at scoring. Therefore, I have recorded the lyrics only. These are my Book of Psalms (Songs). Just as the Bible's Psalms have been recorded without the music scores, whereby each individual singer (believer) can allow the music of their own salvation to "sing" the psalm within them, so too my Book of Songs allows each believer to create his or her own music, beat, and tempo to manifest one's own harmonious walk in the Spirit.

Use them in your devotion times. Use them in your worship – whether individually or when assembled with other believers. In so doing, you too will discover and be able to tell anyone who asks, *The Reason Why I Sing*.

Table of Contents

Table of Contents (cont'd)

Stand Fast

Stand fast and see Yahweh's glory

Stand fast
And see Him reign
Stand fast
And look to Yahoshua
Stand fast
For He's coming again

He took me up
And showed me a better place
He said I'll be with you
And I'll help you to run this race

So, stand fast

There's No One like Yahoshua

With this pen I write
To tell of the Savior
No one in this world
Can liken unto His majesty

Look to Yahoshua for salvation
He shed His blood on a tree
Heed His words He speaks to you
There's no one like Him

Put your trust in His hands
They took the nails for you
Always abound in His love
There's no one like Yahoshua

As red as the ink is upon this page
His blood poured forth
So that we might live eternally
There's no one like Yahoshua

You might think it strange
To glorify what we haven't seen
But His love and sacrifice
Is all the proof I need

There's No One like Yahoshua (cont'd)

When I should die
Please remember His love in me
The light is a dark place
There's no one like Yahoshua

Prayer of Israel

Forgive me, Yahweh

Heal me, Yahweh

Hear me, Yahweh

Save me, Yahweh in Yahoshua' Name

Teach me, Yahweh

Show me, Yahweh

Speak to me, Yahweh

Fill me, Yahweh in Yahoshua Name

Walk with me, Yahweh

Talk with me, Yahweh

Lead me, Yahweh

Use me, Yahweh in Yahoshua Name

Help me, Yahweh

Keep me, Yahweh

Thank you, Yahweh

I love you, Yahweh in Yahoshua Name

Amen.

Psalm 40:1

I need your Spirit in me
I need you Yahweh to make me free
Oh, nothing can save me now but you
I finally know it Yahweh it's true

Oh, Pick me up and set my feet,
Plant them Yahweh on solid ground
I know you'll never leave me Yahweh
You said I'll always be around

Help me Yahweh to make it through
And tell me Yahweh just what to do
I place my life within your hands
Show me Yahoshua, all your plans

Give me patience, peace, and love
Born of wings of the heavenly dove
So I can wait to know your will
And you to say, "Peace be still"

Soul is Saved, Satisfied

Verse 1: No more worries
No more fears
Troubles may come
And they may bring tears
But I've got Yahoshua on my side
He's my Savior and I'm His bride

Chorus: Soul is saved, satisfied
Soul is saved, satisfied
Soul is saved, satisfied
My soul is saved
And I'm satisfied

Verse 2: I've got that oil
To carry me through
The Holy Ghost power
That makes me new
He washed my sins and fears away
Love shines through
So I'm here to say

Chorus
(Repeat from Verse 2)

Author and Finisher of My Faith

Choir: Yahoshua is the author and finisher of my faith
(Repeat 4 xs)

He who has begun a good work in you
Trust in Him and He will see it through

Believe in His saving grace until the end
Though all forsake you He'll be your friend

Yahoshua is the author and finisher of my faith
(Repeat)

I'm baptized with His blood in His name
Old man's crucified, I'm not the same

Holy Ghost power cam on me
Praise His name 'cause now I'm set free

Choir: Yahoshua is the author and finisher of my faith
(Repeat 4 xs)

Sopranos: Author and Finisher
Author and Finisher of my faith
(Repeat)

Author and Finisher of My Faith (cont'd)

Altos & Tenors: Author of my Faith
Finisher of my Faith
Author of my Faith
Finisher of my Faith
(Repeat)

Choir: Yahoshua is the author and finisher of my faith
(Repeat 4 xs)

He who has begun
He who has begun
A good work in you

He will see it through
He will see it through
A good work in you
(Repeat)

Author of my Faith
Finisher of my Faith
(Repeat 3 times)

Psalm 98

O sing unto the Yahweh a new song
For He has done marvelous things
O sing unto the Yahweh a new song
And you'll see the joy that it brings

O He has made know his salvation
His righteousness is open to sight
O praise Him with joyful elation
And others will see His great light

Refrain: Rejoice, now, sing praises
Make a joyful noise all the earth
Rejoice, now, sing praise
For victory comes through rebirth

Let the trumpet sound
Let the haps rejoice
Sound the comet (or cornet) to Him
Let the earth hear your voice

And the son will roar
And the floods clap their hands
For the Yahweh, He will judge
All people and lands

No One like Yahweh

Chorus: There is no one
    No one like Yahoshua
    No one like Yahoshua
    No one like my Yahweh
He can be the Father
He can be the Son
When the Holy Ghost comes upon you
You'll know Messiah is the one

I feel Him in my soul
Can't you hear my spirit moan
Oh, precious Yahoshua
Come and take me home

Chorus

I believe He was
I believe that He is
I believe He shall be
For every eye to see

He's coming back
Coming back for me
Shout Hallelujah
Praise Yahweh! Victory!

Yochanan (John) 14:1-6

I will come again
I will come some day
I will come again, my child
So watch, be ready, and pray

Let not your heart be troubled
Neither let it be afraid
In my Father's House are many mansions
And a place for you I have laid

For I go to prepare a place for you
And I will come again
So that where I am you may be
For I call you more than friend

Where I go, my child, you know
And yes, you know the way
For I am the way, the truth, the life
My blood, has left no sin to pay

So my peace I leave with you
But not as the world might give
I leave the Holy Ghost in you
My child so you might live

Born Again

Chorus: You must be born again
You must be born again
You must be born again
My friend
(Repeat)

Lead: Will you be with us
When the Yahweh comes again
When He comes
Will you be there?

Our lives are but a whisper
One day you're here and then you're gone
But you can live a holy life
When you make Yahoshua your number one

Chorus: You must be born again
You must be born again
You must be born again
My friend
(Repeat)

Born Again (cont'd)

Lead: I know it seems so strange
The things that I talk about
But if you listen to His Spirit
In your heart there won't be a doubt

Won't you come to Him today?
He'll save your soul in a special way
Just tell Him Yahweh, forgive my sin
Yes Yahweh, I want to be born again

Chorus: You must be born again
You must be born again
You must be born again
My friend

When I Feel His Spirit

(1) *Chorus:* I feel the Spirit

I feel it move

When I feel the Spirit

My Soul can't refuse

It moves deep within me

I feel it coming out

When I feel the Spirit

I can't help but jump and shout

(Repeat Chorus)

(2) **Change***:* Move inside, move inside

Move inside of me

(Repeat)

(3) **Sopranos***:* Move inside of me (4 x's)

Altos: Move inside, move inside

Move inside of me

(Repeat)

Tenors: Move, Spirit, Move (4 x's)

(4) All voices simultaneously--their respective parts!

(5) **Change**: Back to (1)

When I Feel His Spirit (cont'd)

(6) *Chorus:* I feel the Spirit (4 x's)

Can <u>you</u> feel the Spirit? (4 x's)

(7) **S & A's:** Brothers, can you feel the Spirit?

Tenors: Yes, we can feel the Spirit!

Sisters, can you feel the Spirit!

S & A's: Yes, we can feel the Spirit!

Speak Through Me

Chorus: Speak through me, Yahweh
Speak through me, Yahweh
Speak through me, Yahweh
Speak through me, Yahweh (repeat)

I know you love me, Yahweh
And you always have
Thanks for helping me to see
Thanks Yahweh, for eye salve

I want to tell them all about you
I want them to know your name
Speak the words so they can hear
Before you come again

Chorus
Yahoshua died on on a tree
He came to save your soul
He rose again that third day
So He could take control

You need to repent of all your sins
So He can take you in
He's waiting for you with open arms
Your heart He wants to win

Speak Through Me (cont'd)

Chorus

1. **Sopranos**: Speak through me, Yahweh

    Speak through me, Yahweh

    Speak through me, Yahweh

    Speak through me, Yahweh

All put together (4 x's - after Tenors come in do their part)

    Speak through me – Yahweh!

2. **Altos**: (come in) Speak through me, Yahweh

3. **Tenors**: (come in) Speak through me, Yahweh

    (4 x's)

    Speak through me, Yahweh

Nothing but the Truth

Lead: Matthew tell us the story
The same one you told the Hebrews
Who rebelled and would not listen
When you tried to share the news

That Yahoshua is the true Messiah
Messiah he is and King of Kings
Even one other King named Martin
Knew through Yahoshua freedom rings

Chorus: Nothing But the Truth so help me Yahweh
Nothing But the Truth so help me Yahweh
Nothing, nothing, nothing but The Truth
Oh, nothing but The Truth so help me Yahweh
(Repeat)

Lead: Mark was the first to testify
To the believers who lived in Rome
Of Yahoshua, a servant on the move
Travelling miles from His home

Healing the sick and feeding the poor
Accepting all who would come
He taught and worked many miracles
So that countless souls were won

Nothing but the Truth (cont'd)

Chorus *(repeat 2 xs)*

Lead: Luke gave us details, an accurate account
Of the salvation that Yahoshua gives
Born of a virgin and the Holy Spirit
The perfect man, our Savior lives

Baptized of "one crying in the wilderness"
One unworthy to unlatch his shoes
Who knew he must decrease while He increase
As a dove signified who Yahweh would use

Chorus

Lead: Yochanan testified in the beginning was the word
And the same was with Yahweh and was Yahweh
Yahoshua, Holy Master of all creation,
Preached repentance wherever He trod

Saying, "I am the Light of the world"
The Life, the Way, the Truth, the Gate
Cease from sin and keep His commandments
Watch, be ready, take heed, and wait!

Nothing but the Truth (cont'd)

Chorus: Nothing but The Truth so help me Yahweh
Nothing but The Truth so help me Yahweh
Nothing, nothing, nothing, but The Truth
Oh, nothing but The Truth so help me Yahweh
(Repeat)

Just give me The Truth (so help me Yahweh)
And nothing but The Truth (nothing else, Yahweh)
(Repeat)

Just give me The Truth, Yahweh (softly)
(Repeat 3 times)

Just give me The Truth, Yahweh (loudly)
(Repeat 3 times)

Just give me The Truth! (Hold high note)

Yahweh's Answer

In My Name
I cleanse your sins
And will change old to new
I heal your infirmities
And all that wars within you
I hear your prayer and ask
That you be born again
My blood shall cover you
From this day forth
And protect you to the end.

In My Name
I give you my word--old and new
All of it surely testifies
They are examples and ensamples
Of things to come--
Assuring my word never dies
Test every spirit when
I make known my will
As a sign, you will speak
With other tongues
As the Holy Spirit's power
Does fill.

Yahweh's Answer (cont'd)

In My Name
I am with you always
And will direct your path
Do all that is pleasing
To forsake my wrath
I seek a vessel
That is tried in the fire
One who'll work with a
Diligent heart
That is the vessel which I desire
A clean, pure, and holy temple
Is where I reside--
One, obedient and faithful--
Not even a jot or a tittle to hide

In My Name
Know that before you ask
Deliverance is on its way
And I chasten my sheep
When they willfully go astray
Your needs are not great
That I cannot fulfill
Know that I AM YAHWEH
And all ye waiting hearts
BE STILL.

I Will Call Your Name

In the morning, Yes Yahweh
In the morning, Yes Yahweh
In the afternoon, Yes Yahweh
I will call your name
I will call your name
I will call your name
Yes Yahweh (repeat)

Yes Yahweh, Yes Yahweh
Yes Yahweh, Yes Yahweh
I will call your name

In the morning, Yes Yahweh
In the morning, Yes Yahweh
I will call your name

I will call your name
In the afternoon
I will call your name
In the afternoon
I will call your name

I will call your name (soprano)
I will call your name (alto)
I will call your name (tenor)
I will call your name (all & hold)

I Will Call Your Name (cont'd)

Father, Father, I will call your name

Messiah Yahoshua, I will call your name

Holy Spirit, I will call your name

I will call your name

Yahweh, Lift Me Up

Yahweh, lift me up
Yahweh, fill my cup
Yahweh, lift me up
Yahweh, fill my cup
Yahweh, lift me higher
Higher than I've ever been
Yahweh, fill me up
Fill me, Yahweh
Once again

What I Can Do

I'm standing for you
I'm standing for you
I'm standing for you
I'm standing for you
Standing, standing, standing for you
I'm praying for you
I'm praying for you
I'm praying for you
I'm praying for you
Praying, praying, praying for you
But I can't live for you
I can't live for you
I can't live for you
I can't live for you
That is something you must do

Anoint Me, Yahweh

Anointing, fall on me

Anointing, fall on me

Yahweh, let your Spirit fall on me

Anointing, fall on me

Anointing, fall on us

Anointing, fall on us

Yahweh, let your Spirit fall on us

Anointing, fall on us

Anointing, cleanse my soul

Anointing, cleanse my soul

Yahweh, let your Spirit cleanse my soul

Anointing, cleanse my soul

Anointing, purge my sins

Anointing, purge my sins

Yahweh, let your Spirit purge my sins

Anointing, purge my sins

Anointing, work In me

Anointing, work in me

Yahweh, let your Spirit work in me

Anointing, work in me

Anointing, show me my call

Anointing, show me my call

Yahweh, let your Spirit show me my call

Anointing, show me my call

Move On In Faith

Unite us Yahweh and bind us as one

Oh Yahweh, we've only begun

We've been rooted and grounded and shown how

There's no stopping us now

We're going to move on, move on, move on in faith

Move on in faith

Open To Yahoshua

Open my eyes, Yahweh
I want to see Yahoshua
Open my eyes, Yahweh
I want to see Him
Open to my ears, Yahweh
So I can hear your voice
Open my lips, Yahweh
So I can rejoice
Open my heart, Yahweh
And teach me to love
Open my mind, Yahweh
To your knowledge above

Yahoshua, My Everything

Today I saw somebody who looked just like you
Yahweh, he talked like you too, so I thought it was you
But as I searched the scriptures down on my knees
Begging you please, Yahweh show me the truth
I need your truth
Now I know you Yahweh, I know for myself
And there is no one else who can lead me astray
Not this day
You are everything,
Yahoshua everything is you in my life
You are everything, Yahoshua everything is you
You're everything, everything, everything to me
I am just convinced that you Yahweh are real
Because your Spirit I feel and He lives in me, yes in me
And I'm no longer shy and I can boldly say
That now I am saved in the gospel way
You are everything,
Yahoshua everything is you in my life
You are everything, Yahoshua everything is you
You're everything, everything, everything to me
I love you Yahweh, with all of my heart,
My soul and my mind
And with all of my strength

Yahoshua, My Everything (cont'd)

And when I hear your voice, I have no choice
But to follow you for the rest of my days
You are everything,
Yahoshua everything is you in my life
You are everything, Yahoshua everything is you
You're everything, everything, everything to me

It's in Your Hands, Yahweh

Healing is in your hands

Healing is in thy hands

Healing is in thy hands, oh Yahweh, it's in your hands

Love is in thy hands

Love is in thy hands

Love is in thy hands;

Peace is in thy hands

Peace is in thy hands

Peace is in thy hands;

Joy is in thy hands

Joy is in thy hands

Joy is in thy hands;

Yahoshua, it's in thy hands

Yahoshua, it's in thy hands

Yahoshua, it's in thy hands;

Here I Am, Send Me

Yahweh looked and He said

My harvest is plentiful

Yea, I need laborers

Oh, I need those who will do my will

And I said Yahweh, Oh Yahweh

Here I am, Oh, here I am

Here I am, send me

So the Spirit of Yahweh is upon me

Because He has anointed me

To preach good tidings, oh, oh

unto the meek

He sent me, oh yes, He has sent me

To bind the broken-hearted

And to proclaim liberty

To the captives to the captives in sin

He has sent me to open the doors of freedom

To them, to them, to them, that are bound

He has sent me

He has sent me

He has sent me

And not myself

Cause I wanted to worship Him

And I wanted to please Him

And I wanted to do His will

Here I Am, Send Me (cont'd)

So I said Yahweh

Here I am

Here I am

Here I am

Send me

Here I am, Yahweh

Here I am, Yahweh

Here I am

Send me

Yahoshua Lifted Me Up

Yahoshua lifted me up
When I was falling down
Then He changed my life
Totally turned it upside down
He said this is the way
My child, so walk herein
And I will be with you
I'll be with you till the end
So, come on, praise His name
He's worthy to be praised
Come on, praise His name
Yes, He's worthy to be praised

Nothing Can Keep Yahweh from Me

Ain't no mountain high enough

Ain't no river wide enough

Ain't no valley low enough

To keep Yahweh from me

(repeat)

Just call His name and you don't have to worry

Just call His name, He'll be there in a hurry

Just say Yahoshua, and He's right there

Just say Yahoshua, and He's right there

Say wash me Yahweh, clean me through and through

Wash me Yahweh, I want to be just like you

Cause there ain't no mountain high enough

Ain't no river wide enough

Ain't no valley low enough

To keep Yahweh from you

And there ain't no mountain high enough

Ain't no river wide enough

Ain't no valley low enough

To keep Yahweh from me

I just call His name, and I don't have to worry

I just call His name, and he's there in a hurry

I say Yahoshua, and He's right there

I say Yahoshua, and He's right there

Nothing Can Keep Yahweh from Me (cont'd)

Cause there ain't no mountain high enough

Ain't no river wide enough

Ain't no valley low enough

To keep Yahweh from me

A Wanderer's Theme Song

My heritage, my land
A place to call my own
I don't know why I wandered
I wandered around so long
My heritage, my land
What I needed so desperately
Was obedience to Yahweh in Messiah
My allegiance to Yahweh in Messiah
Yes, to return to Yahweh in Messiah
To live eternally in me

Our Heritage

Our heritage, our home
And we're one big family
And he gave us a gentle shepherd
Who rules with grace and sovereignty
Our heritage, our home
And we're one big family
And we will work together
And we will pray together
So we can worship in unity

Yahweh's Kingdom

Yahweh's Kingdom, Yahweh's home
He made us one big family
With Yahoshua as our gentle pastor
To unite us in harmony
Yahweh's Kingdom, Yahweh's home
He rules over our big family
And we make disciples
As we praise His name
And of His mighty word
We're never ashamed
For one day we'll live with Him eternally

Out of the Mouth of Babes

People are people
Whatever they do
Just make sure their faults
Don't become a part of you
Yahoshua is the answer
For the world today
He'll help you though
If you only learn to pray
Trust in Yahweh
With all of your heart
That's when you know
You're truly smart
Yahoshua is the answer
Yahoshua is the answer
For the world today
He'll help you though
If you only learn to pray

The Light in the Darkness

Yahoshua, you're the light in the darkness
You're the warmth in the cold
And you knew me even before I was born
So I know you'll be with me when I'm old
And I will praise your name
I'll praise your name
I will praise your holy name
And I will praise your name
I'll praise you name
I will praise your holy name

Do You Have a Testimony?

Do you have a testimony to tell

Has Yahweh fixed you up and made you well

Has He lifted you this day

Has He shown you a better way

Do you have a testimony to tell

Do you have a praise report to give

Has He taught you a better way to live

Has He done something for you

That no one else could do

Do you have a praise report to give

Do you have a testimony to tell

Is it overflowing in you like a well

Then don't just sit there in your seat

Won't you tell us how Yahweh's been sweet

Do you have a testimony to tell

Yahoshua, the Cornerstone

He was rejected of men, rejected of men
For all the eyes to see
And I know how He felt
Because I know how I wept
When they all rejected me
The stone that the builders rejected
Has become the cornerstone
And He makes intercession for you and for me
And He'll never leave us alone
Yahoshua the Cornerstone
You, Messiah, are my cornerstone
So when men reject you
Just say, Yahweh I need you
And just hold your head up high
And He'll lift you up
And He'll fill your cup
And He'll help you to get by
The stone that the builders rejected
Has become the cornerstone
And He makes intercession for you and for me
And He'll never leave us alone, Yahoshua the Cornerstone
You Messiah, are my cornerstone
You Messiah, are my cornerstone
Yahoshua, the cornerstone

Yahweh is my Shepherd

Yahweh is my shepherd

I shall not want

I shall not lack any good thing

To Yahoshua Messiah

I lift my voice

To Him only do I sing

Yahweh is the Good Shepherd

And he leads me

He opens my eyes

And finally I see

Whenever I look over my shoulder

To the left I see Goodness

To the right I see Mercy

And I know they are always behind me

For Yahweh is my shepherd

I shall not want

I shall not lack any good thing

Move, Spirit, Move

I feel the Holy Spirit
I feel it move
When I feel His Spirit
My soul can't refuse
I feel it coming out
When I feel His Spirit
I can't help but jump and shout
Move, Spirit, move
Move inside of me
Oh, move, Spirit, move
Move inside of me

His Name is Yahoshua

Chorus: His name is Yahoshua (3 x's)
Yahoshua, my Messiah

His name is Justice
His name is Mercy
His name is Everlasting Love, Peace, and Joy

Oh call upon Him
He'll always answer
He's there for every woman, man, girl and boy

Chorus

If you don't know Him
It's time to know Him
Time you went on down in Yahoshua's name

Tell Satan goodbye
I'm gone forever
I've been free since the Holy Ghost done came

Yahoshua Is My Song

Yah – ho – shua
Yah – ho – shua
To thee I sing; Let freedom ring
Yah – ho – o – shua

Yah – ho – shua
Yah – ho – shua
This time I know and I won't let go
Yah – ho – o – shua

Yah – ho – shua
Yah – ho – shua
You died for me to set me free
Yah – ho – o – shua

Yah – ho – shua
Yah – ho – shua
No more a slave to the ones from the cave
Yah – ho – o – shua

Yah – ho – shua
Yah – ho – shua
I belong to you though one of the few
Yah – ho – o – shua

Yah – ho – shua
Yah – ho – shua
I finally found COFAH; sing HALLELUYAH!
Yah – ho – o – shua!

The Seed of Abraham

Oh create in me a clean heart
A clean heart is what I need
Oh create in me a clean heart
That's the prayer of Abraham's Seed

Our fathers disobeyed you
And for this sin we were cursed
The nations would rule over us
So unto them we were dispersed

Oh create in me a clean heart
A clean heart is what I need
Oh create in me a clean heart
That's the prayer of Abraham's Seed

The prophets came to warn us
To preach judgment from Yahweh
But the people would not listen
And the Savior they would slay

Oh create in me a clean heart
A clean heart is what I need
Oh create in me a clean heart
That's the prayer of Abraham's Seed

Oh Father please forgive us
For we know not what we do
There can be no true salvation
Until our hearts turn back to you

Oh create in me a clean heart
A clean heart is what I need
Oh create in me a clean heart
That's the prayer of Abraham's Seed

The Seed of Abraham (Cont'd)

Oh Zion, sing praises
Sing praises once again
For the Father has redeemed us
With his mighty outstretched hand

Oh create in me a clean heart
A clean heart is what I need
Oh create in me a clean heart
That's the prayer of Abraham's Seed

About The Author

Elisheva Yaakova (aka Elizabeth James) is a Servant of Yahweh the Most High and has been President and Founder of Fast And Indispensable Temporary Help (F.A.I.T.H.) Ministries, Inc. since February, 1999. She is also the Editor-in-Chief of FM Publishing Company. After 10 other colleges, she has a doctorate in Theology & Biblical Counseling, a master's in Education, bachelor's degree in English, and major course work in many other disciplines. Some of these colleges include: Arizona State University, Phoenix Bible College & Seminary, University of Phoenix, University of Southern California, and Phoenix College. Elisheva Yaakova recognizes that men care about degrees and titles, and therefore, thought it necessary to fulfill this requirement; however, she has come to understand that Yahweh cares nothing about titles and degrees, and that Yahoshua and his disciples were never degreed, yet they preached the word with forthright boldness and through the power of the Spirit of Yahweh.

Elisheva Yaakova says she was born a teacher. She has taught Bible-centered education for 14 years, public education for 8 years, Business and Technology for 8 years, and GED classes for 9 years. In addition, the author is a business owner, divorced mother of two adult children who she raised by herself for 20 years. She owns and operates Geri Lorraine Enterprises, LLC which provides consulting, business services, and grant writing to businesses, non-profits, and schools.

Elisheva Yaakova lived in Coolidge, Arizona most of her younger years and was born in Florence, Arizona. She grew up in the metropolitan L.A. area (Compton, California), and after receiving her call to the ministry 24 years ago and fulfilling her obedience to Yahweh, she returned to Arizona. It is only since 2010 that she has learned a great deal about her true heritage, roots, and identity to recognize that she is one of the descendants of the Black Hebrew Israelites who know that the one they called Yahoshua was really dark-skinned and whose real name is Messiah Yahoshua. She says that although she was baptized in the Baptist Church in 1965, she did not really know Yahoshua, what his sacrifice meant for her, and the true road to eternal life. She celebrated her rebirth in Yahoshua and accepted him as her Messiah on March 31, 1987.

About The Author (cont'd)

Elisheva Yaakova was born Lorraine Juniel. She has published several titles under the name of Lorraine Juniel, E.A. James, and Elizabeth James, and has been a freelance writer for 35 years. In 1996 she won the Diamond Homer Trophy for her poem, *Acquired Taste*. The same year she was awarded the $1,000 Poets of the Year Award for *Tears for Molly*. She wrote under the pen name of Elizabeth Abigail James for many years until December 3, 2010, the day she legally changed her name. Elisheva Yaakova says, through prayer, Yahweh inspired her to change her name to those three Biblical names. Her names in Hebrew are: Elisheva (Elizabeth) Avigayil (Abigail) Yaakova (James). She is the author of 11 other titles which include nonfiction, fiction, poetry, songs, and screenplays. Elisheva Yaakova says writing, like teaching, is not just something she does; a writer, like a teacher, is what she is.

Works and Publications by the Author

A Jealous God, FM Publishing Company, 2010, ISBN 9781931671095 (*screenplay, drama*)

Being a Well Body of Believers, 2nd Edition, FM Publishing Company, 2011. ISBN 9781931671229 (*nonfiction, Biblical counseling*)

Being a Well Body of Believers (6x9 Edition), FM Publishing Company, 2011. ISBN 9781931671262 (*nonfiction, Biblical counseling*)

Being a Well Body of Believers for Hebrew Ysraylites, FM Publishing Company, 2011. ISBN 9781931671347 (*nonfiction, Biblical counseling*)

Being a Well Body of Believers for Hebrew Ysraylites (6x9 Edition), FM Publishing Company, 2010. ISBN 9781931671354 (*nonfiction, Biblical counseling*)

Spiritual Cosmetics for the Soul, *God's Top Beauty Secrets & Grooming Tips for Everlasting Spiritual Health,* 52-Week Devotional for Men and Women **(6x9 Edition),** FM Publishing Company, 2010, ISBN 9781931671224 (*nonfiction, Bible devotionals*)

Spiritual Cosmetics for the Soul, *God's Top Beauty Secrets & Grooming Tips for Everlasting Spiritual Health,* 52-Week Devotional for Men and Women **(Journal Writing & Instruction Edition),** FM Publishing Company, 2010, ISBN 9781931671187 (*nonfiction, Bible devotionals*)

Spiritual Cosmetics for the Soul, *Yahweh's Top Beauty Secrets for Everlasting Spiritual Health,* Devotionals Designed Especially for Hebrew Ysraylite Women **(Small Edition),** FM Publishing Company, 2010, ISBN 9781931671323 (*nonfiction, Bible devotionals*)

Spiritual Cosmetics for the Soul, *Yahweh's Top Beauty Secrets for Everlasting Spiritual Health,* Devotionals Designed Especially for Hebrew Ysraylite Women **(Journal Writing & Instruction Edition),** FM Publishing Company, 2010, ISBN 978193161330 (*nonfiction, Bible devotionals*)

Works and Publications by the Author (cont'd)

The Last Visitor, FM Publishing Company, 2010 (ISBN 9781931671019), Lighthouse Publishing (ISBN 9780979786303) *(fiction, literary, historical romance)*

This Hill I Climb – The Complete Volume (2nd Edition), A Poetic Journey on the Road to Salvation, FM Publishing Company, 2010, ISBN 9781931671316 *(book of poetry)*

This Hill I Climb – The Complete Volume, 2nd Edition, *A Poetic Journey on the Road to Salvation,* FM Publishing Company, 2010, ISBN 9781931671316 *(book of poetry)*

This Hill I Climb, Part One – In the Valley, FM Publishing House, 2001, FM Publishing Company, 2010, ISBN 9781931671026 *(book of poetry)*

This Hill I Climb, Part Two – Climbing, Slipping, and Sliding, FM Publishing House, 2001, FM Publishing Company 2010, ISBN 9781931671033 *(book of poetry)*

This Hill I Climb, Part Three – On the Mountaintop, FM Publishing House, 2001, FM Publishing Company 2010, ISBN 9781931671040 *(book of poetry)*

This Hill I Climb, Part Four – Reaching Back, FM Publishing House, 2001, FM Publishing Company 2010, ISBN 9781931671057 *(book of poetry)*

The Reason Why I Sing, 2nd Edition, FM Publishing Company, 2010, ISBN 9781931671309 *(book of lyrical songs)*

Unforgettable, FM Publishing Company, 2010, ISBN 9781931671101 *(screenplay, drama)*

Why I Should Hate Men, But Don't, FM Publishing Company, 2010, ISBN 9781931671002 *(nonfiction, collection of biographical essays)*

Will Work for Food, Family & Freedom, FM Publishing House, 2009, FM Publishing Company, 2010, ISBN 9781931671064 *(nonfiction, collection of biographical essays)*

With These Hands, FM Publishing Company, 2010, ISBN 9781931671125 *(screenplay treatment, drama)*

Publication and Catalog Ordering Information

To order books, subscribe to the monthly devotionals on audio, get a catalog, or to inquire about screenplay production rights:

Order online at: www.fmpublishingcompany.com

Phone: 877-392-3906

Email: fmpublishing@cox.net

Fax: 520-208-9786

FM Publishing Co.